Working with your Foreign Language Assistant

Robin Page

Head of Modern Languages, Patchway High School

ALL/MGP ·

Mary Glasgow Publications

Designed by Ennismore Design, London
Illustration by Linda Jeffrey
Series Editor: Julie Green
Executive Editorial Consultant for the Association of Language Learning:
    Michèle Deane
Printed and bound in Great Britain by The Baskerville Press, Salisbury, Wiltshire

© Mary Glasgow Publications 1997
An imprint of Stanley Thornes (Publishers) Ltd.
Ellenborough House
Wellington Street
CHELTENHAM
GL50 1YW

A catalogue record for this publication is available from the British Library.

ISBN 0 7487 3031 1

97 98 99 00 01 / 10 9 8 7 6 5 4 3 2 1

The *Concepts* series:

Concepts 1 Using the Target Language by Carol Macdonald
Concepts 2 Appraisal for Language Teachers by Michael
    Pennington
Concepts 3 Managing the Modern Languages Classroom by
    Amanda Flint and Anna Lise Gordon
Concepts 4 Teaching and Learning Grammar by Alison Taylor
Concepts 5 Working with your Student Teacher by Mike
    Calvert and Sarah Fletcher
Concepts 6 Being a Head of Department by Amanda Flint and
    Anna Lise Gordon
Concepts 7 Creativity by Ann Miller
Concepts 8 Developing Advanced Reading Skills in Modern
    Foreign Languages by Ann Barnes and Bob Powell
Concepts 9 Working with your Foreign Language Assistant by
    Robin Page

Contents

About the author

Robin Page is currently Head of Modern Languages at Patchway High School, Almondsbury, South Gloucestershire. He previously worked for two years as an Advisory Teacher for Modern Languages in the former county of Avon. His particular responsibility in that post was for the induction and training of the county's foreign language assistants and newly qualified teachers. He also organised in-service courses on a wide variety of areas for other modern language teachers.

Introduction

The Association for Language Learning is the major UK subject teaching association for all involved in the teaching of modern foreign languages at all levels of education. With over 6,000 members, the Association actively promotes good practice in language teaching and learning through a range of services to members. As well as its journals and newsletters disseminated to members and libraries worldwide, the Association has a publishing programme designed to help teachers and learners to acquire new skills in order to support changing practices and policies.

The *Concepts* series has marked a new phase in the activities of the Association for Language Learning. It has been welcomed as a noteworthy addition to the services that the Association offers to its existing members. The combination of the publishing expertise of Mary Glasgow Publications with the practical and professional knowledge of ALL guarantees that this series of books meets the needs of practising teachers across the various educational sectors and in all parts of the UK.

It is our intention that the books in this series provide positive and constructive guidance for the classroom practitioner. The busy working life of teachers makes it essential for the texts to be accessible and direct. We hope that you, the reader, will find both realism and inspiration within the pages of this book and in the rest of the *Concepts* series.

Michèle Deane
Executive Editorial Consultant, ALL

Foreword

This handbook offers practical advice to teachers and heads of modern languages departments on how to make the best possible use of the time and skills of their Foreign Language Assistant (FLA). Since the FLA will only be in the department for a matter of months, and only perhaps for a few hours per week, it is essential to train them quickly and effectively so that optimum use can then be made of the limited time available. This handbook suggests ways of rapidly integrating the FLA into a school and the department so that subsequent language activities with students take place smoothly in an atmosphere of confidence in which the FLA shares and understands the objectives of his/her colleagues.

The initial chapters deal with issues of induction and on-going training. They are followed by chapters in which practical suggestions are made for the sorts of activities in which the FLA can be involved to the benefit of both students and teaching colleagues. Case studies are given at appropriate points in the book to illustrate the advice or the activities under discussion. Sample activities are provided both within chapters and in an appendix. The essential emphasis of the book is on helping each FLA, with their own individual strengths, to reach their full potential in the modern languages department as rapidly as possible so that students will gain maximum benefit from this unique member of the school's languages team.

It is accepted that different schools will want to make their own specific arrangements for the deployment of their FLAs and this book aims to give a variety of suggestions which are applicable to a wide range of teaching situations throughout all the Key Stages. Many schools are now sharing FLAs since other budgetary priorities have made it impossible for them to employ full-time assistants – the advice and ideas in this book are relevant to both of these cases.

What if your school does not have a Foreign Language Assistant?

Since many schools do not yet benefit from the special services of an FLA, I have included in Appendix 1 (page 26) a brief description of the work of the FLA taken from a recent promotional leaflet from the National Association of Language Advisers. I hope that this will provide strong arguments to help persuade headteachers and their governing bodies of the important contributions which FLAs can make to the curriculum.

I leave the last word in this introduction to the Central Bureau for Educational Visits and Exchanges which has a leaflet on the subject saying that, "a foreign language assistant brings language learning alive" by:

- providing access to a native speaker
- stimulating genuine communication in the target language
- bringing the foreign country and its culture to the classroom
- giving specialist attention to individuals, pairs and groups
- providing a ready source of authentic material
- updating teachers' knowledge of the target language and culture
- bringing an international dimension to the curriculum
- helping to prepare for national examinations
- raising the level of performance in oral examinations.

And all that at the current 1996–7 salary of just £4,628 – please read on!

1 Welcome and induction

Initial contacts

First contacts between the FLA and the school are invariably made towards the end of a very busy summer term. It is usually the head of department who telephones the FLA to "offer" him or her the post, and it is really at this early stage that the process of welcome and induction begins. It is important to convey a positive impression about the school and the job to the FLA on the other end of the telephone. The FLA will be making quite a long commitment to the school and will want to know at least some important facts about the post at this stage. It is perhaps advisable to have some information ready concerning the age range of pupils, the nature of the school and accommodation arrangements for the FLA. Having established that he or she actually wants the job, a follow-up letter can then be sent including more detailed information about the post, the department and the school. The FLA will find the following information useful at this stage:

- details of the geographical situation of the school
- details about the surrounding area
- a copy of the school brochure
- a list of items which he or she could bring from the home country for later use in teaching (see Appendix 2, page 27)
- exact salary details
- the Central Bureau booklet about the post of FLA (this is also sent to all assistants from the Central Bureau with an introductory letter)
- information about accommodation
- some advice on how much money to bring for the first month
- holiday contact numbers and addresses of the teacher(s) responsible for him/her
- contact address of the previous FLA.

WARNING!

Details about schemes of work, teaching methodologies and so on are best saved for face-to-face discussion once the FLA has begun to feel acclimatised – there is no point in sending out the weighty departmental handbook as holiday reading!

You may also need to give advice about travel arrangements, and it is often necessary to have someone from the department meet the FLA on arrival at the local station or airport. Once the FLA has set foot in school, he or she will be entirely dependent on the languages department for help with a whole range of important and practical matters which must be dealt with during the first few days. These include:

- checking that accommodation is suitable
- appointing a colleague to act as "mentor" for the FLA
- helping with banking arrangements
- clarifying situation re income tax, council tax, DSS, etc.
- making sure that the FLA registers with a doctor
- inviting FLA home for a meal or out for a drink!
- making sure FLA has enough money for the first month in school
- explaining arrangements for tea/coffee at school
- explaining arrangements for school meals
- giving FLA a school calendar (holidays, INSET days)
- introducing FLA to headteacher and others

- taking FLA on guided tour of school
- giving FLA a map of the school
- giving FLA a map of the area around the school
- providing FLA with a copy of timetable as soon as possible
- providing FLA with a reasonable room to teach in
- if possible, giving FLA a room key
- giving FLA copies of main course books
- providing FLA with syllabuses, exam papers, etc.
- ensuring he/she knows about FLA induction course (where appropriate)
- giving information on English courses at local further or higher education institutions
- helping with travel arrangements between lodgings and school.

Many departments also like to organise a welcome meal for their FLA – of course, this helps to "break the ice" and will enable the FLA to get to know the other teaching colleagues more quickly. All of these steps are worth taking since they will help the assistant feel welcome and wanted right from the start.

Appointing a mentor

If schools are to ensure that their assistants work effectively, clear arrangements need to be made for overseeing the welfare and integration of the FLA throughout the year. It makes sense for one individual in the modern languages department to take on this responsibility of mentor for the FLA. Where assistants are shared between establishments, it would make sense for each school to provide its own mentor for the FLA and perhaps to organise their timetable in such a way as to ensure that the FLA spends an uninterrupted week in each school rather than trekking backwards and forwards between schools during the same week. The role of the mentor might include:
- making the FLA welcome
- being a friend and adviser
- showing FLA around (school and town)
- helping with administration (DSS, doctor, etc.)
- helping to solve problems
- introducing them to other friends and colleagues
- liaising with the head of department
- listening and explaining to FLA.

In choosing a mentor for the FLA, the head of department could consider the following points:
- it is a very important role
- discuss the role with the rest of the department
- someone might be very keen to do it
- the role could provide a useful staff development opportunity
- a younger teacher might identify more closely with the FLA
- in a large department, you might consider a different mentor for each FLA
- counselling skills will be required
- some non-teaching time will have to be given up.

In selecting the best person for the job, the head of department may have to encourage reluctant, but nevertheless suitable, colleagues to put themselves forward. Conversely, he or she may also have to dissuade unsuitable colleagues from applying. It would be a good principle to publish a list of selection criteria for the job of mentor in advance to ensure that everything is done openly and fairly. In some departments, the position of mentor to FLAs may be part of a package of responsibilities for which an allowance is awarded, while elsewhere it may be seen as a useful but unremunerated professional development opportunity.

You may wish to formalise this support process to some extent by establishing a framework for reviewing the assistant's progress and welfare throughout the year. It will certainly help to provide the FLA with an opportunity to reflect on his or her experiences and to discuss this with the mentor at certain key times in the year. The next chapter deals in more detail with this question of support and monitoring.

Observing lessons

It is essential that FLAs take part in a carefully prepared and guided period of lesson observation before they can fully assume their role within the modern languages department. Far too many assistants arrive in the UK with unrealistic expectations concerning the pupils whom they will be teaching. They often expect to find pupils with a high level of fluency and competence in the foreign language, and in fact they soon discover that language teachers in the UK are sometimes hard-pressed just to motivate their pupils, let alone equip them to become avid readers of those *Nouvel Observateur, Stern* or *El País* magazines which the FLAs have so thoughtfully brought with them in their suitcases!

It is helpful to plan a period of lesson observation in which the FLA sees the whole range of ability and all the language teachers at work. This will enable the assistant to gain an overview of the languages situation in the school and to begin to be aware of a variety of techniques used by different colleagues to motivate and teach their pupils. FLAs are sometimes shocked by the seemingly minimal linguistic input that may take place with some lower ability groups, yet this is a salutary lesson which needs to be learned as early as possible if the FLA is to have appropriate expectations of the pupils.

The period of observation should last at least one week and should also allow for some active involvement by the FLA in some lessons. Suggestions for involvement and participation by the FLA at this stage could include:
- pupils interviewing the FLA
- FLA and teacher staging a dialogue
- FLA participating in a class game prepared by the teacher.

The National Association of Language Advisers (NALA) suggests that at this stage the FLA should be, "actively involved in the lesson for short periods of time as a form of gentle, controlled introduction for their future role".

You may also wish to arrange different patterns of observation for your FLA during this initial period, but remember that they are only in school for twelve hours per week! Possible patterns of observation could include:
- follow one teacher one day, another teacher another day
- follow a variety of teachers on the same day
- observe a range of ability groups within the same year group
- mix observation with some "in-class" support
- follow a class through a morning of lessons in different curriculum areas.

Whichever approach you choose, it would be helpful to spend a short time with the FLA before and after each session, discussing objectives and sharing feedback on what has been seen. You can begin to give a context to lessons observed in terms of communicative language teaching and the many varied strategies which teachers use in order to present, reinforce and practise language structures. At this stage, the FLA should begin to become aware of the differentiated curriculum as it relates to the varying levels of attainment and expectations in the classes observed. Some teachers have become very skilled in providing lesson observation opportunities for the FLA and many provide the assistant with guidance in their observation by giving them specific targets to look for, such as, "in my next Year 9 lesson, I want you to follow the way in which I draw the group's attention to the perfect tense with *être*". Giving a clear focus for classroom observation makes for a much sharper, more concentrated feedback session after the lesson. Many such skills learned through appraisal or through our work with student teachers as part of the I.T.T. schemes are fully transferable to the induction and training of our FLAs.

Courses for the FLA

Some LEAs continue to provide induction and training opportunities for their assistants. Such courses often take the form of an initial whole-day session very early in October, followed perhaps by shorter meetings during the school year. They can be very good value for money, particularly as the FLA's attendance on a course incurs no added supply costs for the school.

The initial "induction course" should provide the FLA with an excellent opportunity to put what he or she has already observed in school into a broader context. Inputs on the current methodologies used in language teaching will make more sense to an FLA who has already experienced some classroom teaching as part of the observation period.

Attendance at the LEA course will also enable assistants to meet one another, to socialise and to discuss their experiences so far in their schools. This informal "networking" is an invaluable spin-off from an externally provided course and will provide the basis for on-going support and cross-fertilisation of ideas between FLAs.

In areas that do not have the luxury of a centrally organised induction course, it is becoming increasingly common to establish a formal system of networking across a cluster of schools. The clusters may be based on the old TVEE consortia or simply formed from schools that are geographically close or whose heads of department are already used to collaborative working. A successful and established pattern for the induction and training of FLAs through networking could follow this model from an LEA in the South East:

- 15 schools (ex-TVEE consortium) participate
- each school contributes £20 to an FLA INSET fund
- one school hosts the initial day for 20–24 FLAs
- inputs are given by speakers from ALL/local language teachers
- video INSET materials are also used
- two language teachers from cluster schools are released to facilitate the day
- subsequent meetings take place in twilight time
- twilight meetings are hosted by schools on a rota basis
- language teachers facilitate twilight meetings on a rota basis.

Whether through a centrally organised course or through a system of networking, the FLA will benefit greatly from the specialised input and the sharing of ideas which come from some form of external induction. A good combination of in-school induction and outside inspiration will equip FLAs to fulfil their role more effectively and more confidently.

Summary

- Making the FLA feel welcome will ensure a smooth start.

- Appointing a mentor will provide support for the FLA.

- A period of induction will provide essential initial training.

2 Further training, support and development

Keeping the FLA involved

The training of your assistant does not end after their period of observation or induction course. Your aim must be to get the most out of this new member of your department. You will only be able to do this if you ensure that the FLA feels fully involved in the work of the department – in short, you must treat the FLA as a fully-fledged colleague, in much the same way as you would treat a newly qualified teacher.

In order to keep your FLA involved, it is important to establish that regular liaison occurs between the assistant and the teachers with whom they are working. Before the FLA can contribute to lessons, he or she needs a clear idea of where the teacher is going with the class so that the FLA's role can be discussed, clarified and understood. This does imply some meeting time between the FLA and the classroom teacher. If you need to use a non-teaching period for this, ensure that you are left free. A regular meeting with the FLA at a fixed time is desirable. Such meetings will probably become briefer and more informal as the FLA and teacher get to know each other better, but some liaison between lessons will always be necessary. It is unreasonable to expect the FLA to magically "slot into" an activity planned by the teacher without some previous knowledge of (or input into) the nature of the activity. It is even more unreasonable for a teacher to fail to involve the FLA in his or her lesson because of a lack of planning or the mistaken conviction that having to think about integrating the FLA into the lesson is just one more unwelcome complication in the already stressful life of a language teacher! If the FLA is allowed some input into the planning of the activities in which they are to be involved, their contribution will be a positive, supportive one which will actually enable the language teacher to enrich the learning experience of the pupils.

Many departments also like to involve their FLAs in at least some department meetings. There will be times at which it is appropriate for the FLA to contribute to discussion and decision-making with the rest of the department. It is important, for example, for the FLA to gain some understanding of National Curriculum levels, and so it would be valuable for him or her to attend meetings at which samples of pupils' work are discussed with reference to the level descriptions. The FLA will also have contributions to make in discussions specifically related to teaching techniques, displays of pupils' work, progress of individual pupils, planning intensive language sessions, and so on. It may be felt less appropriate, however, for the FLA to attend meetings with a more "administrative" content in which the assistant would not have a clear role (or even any interest). What matters is that the FLA should at least feel he or she has the opportunity to be involved in the discussions and decisions which must directly relate to his or her own work within the department.

Follow-up sessions, courses and networking with other FLAs (see Chapter 1) will also supplement the on-going training of the assistant, as will the use of training videos and INSET publications (see page 42 for more details). As the weeks go by, you will also have opportunities to show the FLA other resources, such as CD-Roms, library facilities, listening centres, the IT room, and so on. You should aim to have the FLA involved in all aspects of your language work and able to make use of all your equipment and facilities.

Further lesson observation

The initial period of observation, the induction course and the FLA's first few lessons, either alongside the class teacher or working independently with very small groups, will all have helped to clarify for the FLA both the context within which he or she is working and his or her own special role within that context. In order to build on these foundations, it will be useful for the FLA to have perhaps one lesson of observation per fortnight built into the timetable. The focus of observation could relate to an area or skill which the FLA wants to explore and develop – this focus may arise from the review process referred to in Chapter 1. A mentor or head of department, who is aware of the FLA's wishes or needs, could plan a programme of observation for the FLA in consultation with colleagues. The FLA could be asked to:

- observe the teacher and German assistant team-teaching in order to prepare for a similar activity with a French teacher
- observe a lesson with IT before running a similar lesson independently with a small group
- watch how one teacher teaches "time" with Year 7 before running a revision session on the same topic with Year 9
- compare how two different teachers present the same linguistic structure
- observe how one teacher uses the OHP with one class, before using it later in the week with the sixth form.

The FLA may also benefit from observing lessons in other curriculum areas. This will add to his or her understanding of the whole-school picture as well as enabling him or her to see the same pupils performing in a very different context. It also enhances the FLA's overall cultural understanding of the nature of our education system and the National Curriculum.

A framework for support and development

In Chapter 1 it was suggested that a mentor could provide valuable, on-going support for the assistant. Some schools have found it useful to formalise this support by introducing a framework for regularly reviewing the work and welfare of the FLA.

Such a process has the double advantage of underlining the FLA's entitlement to support and development while at the same time enabling the school to monitor the cost-effectiveness of its investment in terms of the quality of contributions being made to the curriculum by the assistant.

It is suggested that this review process should take the form of a focused dialogue between the FLA and his or her mentor or head of department. It is important to involve your senior management team in the process by asking them to allocate you protected time in which to hold the interview and by also providing feedback to them on how things are going with your FLA(s). In this way you will show your own involvement in the FLA's professional development and also make a vital statement about the importance attached to the assistant's role. Where things are going well, your discussion with the FLA will enable you to identify areas for further development. Where there may be problems, the discussion should help you and your assistant to develop strategies to deal with them. You may also find any notes which you make during this formalised support process useful as a basis for your final report to the Central Bureau as well as for any references which your FLA may request from you.

Case study – The support process in action

This 11–18 Bristol comprehensive school has used a formal "review and development" framework with its assistants for several years. The school shares its French and German FLAs with another local school and also has a one-third share in a Spanish assistant. The review system is based on a termly dialogue between the FLA and the mentor, and the focus for this dialogue is provided by review sheets (see Appendix 3, pages 28–33). Towards the end of each term (or more often if necessary), a "review interview" is arranged to discuss the areas detailed on each review sheet. The basic format for the sheets remains the same for each review, though the initial and final sheets cover areas of specific relevance for the beginning and end of the FLA's year.

How are the reviews carried out?

- The mentor explains the purpose of the review to the FLA and fixes an interview date (in consultation with the senior management team).
- The FLA is given the review sheets a few days before the agreed date – these provide the agenda for the discussion.
- The FLA is encouraged to prepare notes and questions for the discussion.
- The mentor also has a copy of the sheets to complete in order to provide a record of the discussion.
- The summary sheets (see Appendix 3, pages 28–33) are completed with an agreed statement of progress covering the same three areas as the review sheets (Teaching, School Life, Life outside School).
- Agreed areas for "proposed action" are recorded on the summary sheets.
- Copies of the completed summary sheets are given to the FLA and the head of department and kept by the mentor who also feeds back to the senior management team.
- At each subsequent review meeting, the previous areas for "proposed action" are always used as a starting point for discussion in order to see what has been achieved.
- The school finds it useful to "colour code" the sheets so that the various participants in the process have their own readily identifiable sheets.

This school finds that the review is often very helpful in highlighting potential difficulties and suggesting realistic ways forward. How often the process is used, depends very much on the nature of the FLA. Since this school also has to share its FLAs with other schools, the support provided formally by the review discussions also helps the FLA to feel more integrated in a school at which he or she is very much a part-time member of staff. The process has introduced an important element of self-evaluation into the FLA's work which is appreciated by all concerned.

Whole-school issues

During the course of the year, the FLA will come across anomalies and quirks in the UK school system which seem to have no equivalent in his or her home country. An interested FLA (perhaps one who is contemplating a career in teaching) may wish to know more about how pupils are statemented, how our records of achievement are compiled or what really goes on in PSE lessons. A school that runs a training programme for its newly qualified teachers may well cover such topics in its twilight sessions. The FLA could be offered the opportunity to attend seminars along with the NQTs – again, giving a sense of involvement is an important principle.

There is no doubt that the FLA will have to be given clear guidance on whole-school issues such as procedures relating to pupil behaviour. Most of this information (and support) will come directly from the head of department or mentor in the languages department, but there is also a case for the FLAs participating in any briefing sessions which may be run by the senior management team at certain key moments in the school year. The FLA may also wish to attend some staff meetings and morning briefing sessions in order to be kept informed of what is currently happening in the life of the school.

Developing the skills of your FLA

Although your FLA will need guidance, training and support, he or she will also bring special, individual talents to the job and to the host school. It is important that languages colleagues should be able to spot these talents at an early stage and then do everything possible to encourage their development and integration in the work of the FLA. The FLA will feel happy with the freedom to exploit his or her own skills in the new job and the rest of the department may learn new and interesting tricks from their young colleague! Here are two examples of schools which recognised and nurtured the strengths of their FLAs.

Case study 1 – Adding rap to MFL lessons!

In this 11–16 Bath school, the new French FLA was a true devotee of French rap music. He decided to use the medium of rap to liven up the way in which pupils were being asked to practise their role plays. Working in consultation with the teacher, the FLA wrote a list of ten phrases in French for inviting someone out, such as:

> *Tu veux sortir avec moi?*
> *Tu peux venir au cinéma?*
> *T'as envie de sortir ce soir?*

He also compiled a list of ten phrases for turning down the invitation, such as:

> *Non, j'ai pas envie ce soir.*
> *Non, je ne peux pas.*
> *Non merci, pas avec toi.*

The teacher and FLA then worked together with the class, splitting them into two groups but keeping them in the same room. Group 1 were coached by the FLA into setting the ten invitation phrases to a rap beat, while the teacher did the same with Group 2 and the negative phrases. It was then time to put it all together. The "inviting" group began by chanting in chorus their first invitation, followed by the second group chanting their first refusal (keeping to a rap-like rhythm) – and so on until it was over.

The FLA went on to set many GCSE topics to rap music, beating out a simple rhythm or sometimes bringing a music tape into the classroom to accompany the pupils. He also introduced some groups to much more complex language by bringing his genuine rap tapes to school. His colleagues encouraged his initiative and learned a new teaching technique in the process.

Case study 2 – The FLA as artist

None of the language teachers in this 11–18 Bristol comprehensive school had ever got beyond the intricacies of matchstick figures in their artistic education. Their German assistant quickly saw an opportunity for her own very advanced artistic talents and planned with the teachers ways in which she could quickly illustrate in the classroom some of the more tricky words and phrases which the teachers were struggling to explain in the target language. They developed a "double-act" which worked so well that the pupils were disappointed when a lesson had no artistic input. The FLA also taught her colleagues some simple techniques to improve their own artistic achievements.

In both case studies, the FLAs were allowed to develop their own talents in the classroom with the unplanned end result that the teaching colleagues also improved their own hitherto under-developed skills. The FLA can also be a source of planned staff development for those modern language colleagues keen to practise and improve their own language skills. More and more language teachers find themselves having to teach their weaker second (or even third) foreign language to pupils. A substantial number of non-specialist teachers are called upon to teach a language without any previous specialised training and without any recent experience of using the language. Allocating a small proportion of the FLA's timetabled lessons to help such colleagues improve their confidence and competence in the foreign language is increasingly seen as a very valid and valuable use of the available time. An added boost also comes naturally in a department where the members often converse openly and spontaneously in the target language at break-time, lunch-time and around the corridors.

Reaching full potential

The training, support and development opportunities that you provide for your FLA will bring rapid rewards to the modern languages department. Since the FLA will only be in the department for a matter of months, and only in some cases for a few hours per week, it is essential to train them quickly and effectively so that optimum use can then be made of the limited time available. On-going support and training will allow the FLA to be more rapidly integrated into the life of the department. The FLA who is valued as a colleague will also be able to contribute to the staff development of the other modern language teachers in the school.

Summary

- Training the FLA is a continuous process.

- A formalised support process will bring benefits.

- The FLA must be valued as a colleague.

- Teachers can be supported by the FLA.

3 Team-teaching with the FLA

Rationale

Since it is desirable for the learner to be aware of the foreign language as a means of communication, it is important to provide a range of examples of communication in the target language, both planned and spontaneous. If the teacher and FLA work alongside each other in the classroom, this becomes possible in a very natural and effective way. Use of the target language will appear as the obvious means of communication between the FLA and the teacher and the "spin-off" effect on the students will be that they see the language at work between two speakers who are more proficient in the language than themselves. It also encourages them to listen and understand the interchanges and to use the language themselves both in the planned activities of the lesson and in the more spontaneous moments in the classroom (asking to be allowed to open the window, working with a partner, borrowing a pen, etc.). Eavesdropping on the conversations between the FLA and the teacher will enable pupils to pick up new language, to catch snippets of humour and to witness a genuine, "unscripted" dialogue. We all know just how hard it is to teach pupils to use the target language naturally and spontaneously – the more the pupils are exposed to it, the more likely they are to make this leap forward!

Part of the routine

Try to involve the FLA for every moment of the time that he or she spends in the classroom, not just for the main part of the lesson which you have planned together. Greet the FLA in front of the class (even if this means engineering his or her arrival in the room a few seconds after your own) and encourage the pupils and the FLA to greet each other. If your normal routine involves taking the register at the start of the lesson, ask the FLA to do this occasionally. If you prefer to take the register, the FLA can be writing the date on the board or circulating in the room and discreetly encouraging individuals to get their books and equipment ready. Requests for help (in the target language, of course!) may be channelled to the FLA, who can also play an active part in directing pupils to arrange tables and equipment before, during and after activities. At the end of the lesson, the FLA will be there to help with the smooth dismissal of the class and to say "Goodbye" much more authentically and with much more variety than the majority of classroom teachers!

Two teachers are better than one!

In certain situations, the modern languages teacher is hard-pressed to devote adequate time to the individual members of the class – we would all like another pair of hands (as well as eyes and ears) sometimes. The FLA can be a particular bonus in lessons that involve either taking your class out of the classroom for IT and library sessions, or reorganising your class into groups that will take part in a "circus" or carousel of language activities. In such situations, the sorting and allocation of the respective roles of the teacher and FLA must be carefully discussed and agreed in advance – if you are holding a planning meeting in a free period, ask the senior management team to support you by keeping you free from cover that lesson.

Case study 1 – The IT session

In this 11–16 Bristol comprehensive school, each language class has a timetabled session in the school's network room once a month. The head of department has timetabled the FLA to join the class for many of these sessions. The software used is *Fun With Texts, Developing Tray* and *Microsoft Works*. The role of the French or German FLA is to assist pupils by circulating among them, prompting them, answering their questions and explaining why certain words or phrases "fit" while others do not. The FLA is able to offer differentiated support to the pupils, thus enabling them to be more "stretched" by the IT tasks. The teacher performs a similar function, though in addition she is responsible for the timing of activities and for overseeing the lesson. Occasionally the FLA will read texts or sections of text to the pupils, thus adding a listening or dictation element to the IT task. The FLA is asked to speak only in the target language and also to stick to an agreed range of "technical" vocabulary previously discussed with the teacher – this allows the pupils to benefit from a common approach from both FLA and teacher.

Before the lesson, the classroom teacher and FLA meet to discuss the text to be used (or the nature of the word-processing exercise) in order to foresee and plan for any expected difficulties and to decide on any special role to be adopted by either colleague. As well as the teaching function of the FLA, he or she also helps with practical issues such as technical hitches, switching machines on and off correctly and supervising the use of the equipment.

Case study 2 – The library lesson

The languages department in this South Gloucestershire 11–18 comprehensive school has a reading programme which involves every class in Years 8–10 spending one lesson in the school library approximately once every six weeks. Here again, the head of department has managed to timetable the FLA to accompany most classes on their visits to the library. The FLA arrives in the library before the class and the teacher and takes about five minutes to set out the materials which are to be used, taking care to arrange the books on the display table according to the colour-coded levels of difficulty (the books used are *Bibliobus, Lire Davantage, Lesekiste, Lesezeichen, Bücherregal* and Mary Glasgow magazines). Together with the teacher, he or she guides the pupils in their choice of a book, checking their reading records with them to see what they have already covered. Once the reading is underway, both the teacher and FLA go from table to table assisting pupils, asking them to read sections aloud and encouraging them with the follow-up activity at the end of each book. Pupils are trained to use bilingual dictionaries which are kept in the library – again, both the teacher and FLA play a part in this. Some pupils ask to listen to their chosen story on cassette in the adjoining studio – the FLA organises this, and some of the recordings have been made by the school's FLAs while others are purchased from the publisher.

In their library handbooks, pupils are encouraged to review books in the target language, using a range of structures and vocabulary for giving opinions – again, the FLA is on hand to assist in this and to offer support at a level appropriate to the pupil. The FLA chooses pupils to pack away the books at the end of the lesson and also oversees this process.

Before the lesson, the FLA and class teacher have met to decide which books and reading materials should be put out for the class. The teacher will suggest ways in which the FLA can stretch more able pupils and give extra help to the slower readers. The FLA also has suggestions to make which will add a further dimension to the library lesson, offering, for example, to take pairs or small groups of pupils to an adjoining classroom so they can read aloud or act out sections from their chosen books.

Case study 3 – A carousel or "circus" of activities

The head of department of this 11–18 Bristol comprehensive school wanted to practise a variety of skills with her Year 10 German class in relation to the GCSE topic of school life. She devised a range of tasks involving listening, using IT, speaking, reading and playing a sentence-building game. Since all 30 pupils had to complete all five activities in a one-hour lesson, the timing and logistics had to be planned very slickly. The best time to attempt this "circus" or carousel was during the FLA's regular weekly lesson with the class so that he could take responsibility for two of the activities – using IT and speaking.

The teacher decided how to split the class before the lesson and briefed them on their various tasks at the end of the previous lesson. The listening, reading and IT tasks were planned so as to be easy to manage and self-correct, requiring only the minimum of supervision. This left the FLA free to take a very active role in the speaking while the teacher enjoyed playing the sentence game with her groups! As the groups switched activities, both the teacher and FLA ensured that each activity was ready to start up afresh. As in the two previous case studies, the FLA was able to provide differentiated support throughout the activities at a level appropriate to the individuals concerned.

Before the lesson, it had been necessary for the teacher to give the FLA a clear overview of how the activities related to each other and what their respective responsibilities would be. On some occasions, such lessons began with a presentation by the FLA and teacher who covered essential new language in the first ten to fifteen minutes of the lesson. There was still time to follow this with the carousel of three or four ten to fifteen minute activities. The FLA needed to study the materials to be used, though he was already familiar with some of these through his work with other groups. He was confident with the IT activity (using three BBC computers sited at the back of the classroom) because he had trained in this during his first two weeks in the school and had regular opportunities to work with pupils on computers.

Keeping the FLA in your classroom

In the above case studies, the presence of the FLA has enabled the teacher either to take the class out of the classroom for enriching activities or to organise a wider range of classroom-based activities. What of the FLA's potential contribution to some of the more everyday language learning tasks which take place in the classroom? In many instances, the "double-act" between FLA and teacher can do much to emphasise and enhance the interactive nature of language. The following examples show how working with the FLA will take attention away from the teacher, away from the tape-recorder and towards the interaction that is one of the ultimate goals of the foreign language teacher.

▪ Mock interviews

After careful pre-lesson preparation with the teacher, the FLA assumes a false identity in class and it becomes the job of the teacher and pupils to discover this identity. Initially, the teacher asks the questions and then aims to involve the pupils by prompting them, giving clues and so on. Another possibility could involve the FLA posing as a witness to an imaginary crime while the pupils become detectives, noting down the answers to their questions in order to build up a picture of what happened and who did what: "What colour was the car?" "How old was the thief?" "What time was it?"

■ Presentations

Ask the FLA to prepare authentic mini-presentations for the class on subjects such as sport in the home country/region, home town, pop music in Spain, local customs, and so on. The exact length of the presentation will depend on the linguistic level of the class but may be as short as five minutes with a class of beginners or a low ability group and as long as fifteen to twenty minutes with more advanced students. The teacher can prepare the class in advance by helping them to plan questions to ask the FLA. Initial questions can be asked by the teacher acting as prompter. The FLA could be encouraged to bring visual materials, cassettes or video to add interest.

■ The dumb tourist

To present a model dialogue to the class, the teacher takes the stereotyped part of the slightly "slow" British tourist abroad, while the FLA plays the native speaker (waiter, receptionist, police officer, etc.). A well-prepared conversation can be very amusing and will hold the attention of the class more effectively than disembodied voices on a cassette. Both the teacher and FLA could then follow up by helping pupils to prepare and present their own dialogues based on the original model. This should make transactional language fun!

■ Putting the action into interaction!

In order to lead into language activities, you first need to engage your pupils and get them interested in your activity. Why not try staging a carefully planned (but seemingly spontaneous) argument between yourself and the FLA? This provides the opportunity to practise language related to giving opinions in a dramatic way. Other ideas could include:
• prepare a dialogue in which the FLA accuses you of taking something of theirs (descriptions)
• ask the FLA what he or she did at the weekend knowing full well that you have agreed previously that the answers will be silly or outrageous instead of the usual, "I went to the cinema", "I watched TV" and so on.
The possibilities for some dramatic interactions where the classroom audience are fooled (at least temporarily) into suspending disbelief are almost endless.

An atmosphere of confidence

Team-teaching with the FLA does assume an open, trusting relationship between the two partners. It will not work in situations where the FLA (or any other visitor to the classroom) is seen as a threat to the class teacher's autonomy. Some language teachers feel somewhat insecure at the thought of a native speaker overhearing their occasional mispronunciations or slips of grammar – this is particularly true of non-specialist teachers. In a successful languages department, it is hoped that the FLA will not be viewed as a threat but rather as a rich source of contemporary language and culture and therefore as a support to other teaching colleagues. The classroom teacher and the FLA need to establish exactly what sort of team-teaching they both feel comfortable with and clearly agree the roles of each partner in the relationship. In this way, there should not be any unpleasant surprises, but rather the establishment of good working practices in a climate of mutual confidence and respect.

Summary

• Working alongside the FLA makes more adventurous activities possible.

• Working interactively with the FLA provides a model for pupils to follow.

• The FLA is there to support both the teacher and the pupils.

4 The FLA with small groups and individuals

Rationale

In Chapter 3 we saw how the FLA can work alongside the teacher, making pupils aware of the communicative nature of language learning. In a team-teaching situation, the teacher will probably want to remain in control of the activity and will also be able to supervise and support the FLA as part of the double-act. A competent and confident FLA will, however, contribute much to the language learning of the pupils by having regular opportunities to work independently with them in small groups, pairs or with individuals. The FLA can provide a unique opportunity for pupils to be taken out of the classroom in order to enjoy and be involved in follow-up activities that relate closely to the language work covered in normal lessons.

The teacher does not "let go"

This is not to say that the FLA is left completely free to conduct one of the so-called "conversation lessons" of twenty years ago in which a group of tongue-tied pupils would sit for 30 minutes with an embarrassed young foreigner who clearly had no idea of how to involve the pupils or no idea what they had been learning in class. It remains essential for the teacher and the FLA to plan the activities jointly for the session so that the pupils are able to participate with confidence since they will be re-using language presented to them in the classroom.

It is also important to plan the timing of the small-group activity carefully so that groups change over smoothly and with a minimum of fuss. The FLA must also be clear about what constitutes acceptable behaviour and what action to take if there is a problem. If all these conditions are met, the FLA's "mini-lesson" will be a successful extension to the class activity, providing pupils with a chance to participate orally in a more intimate situation than that of whole-class teaching. Proper planning and consultation will ensure that the teacher, although not physically present with the FLA, remains firmly in control of both the class activity and the extension activity. The following case study serves as a possible model.

Case study – A model for the FLA with small groups

This 11–18 South Gloucestershire comprehensive school chooses to employ one full-time French and one full-time German FLA each year. A small seminar room in the modern languages area has been designated the FLA room and is used for sixth form language teaching, as well as for the assistants to use when they are withdrawing small groups from the classroom. The room is large enough for up to twelve pupils at any one time and it has a flip-chart, display boards on two of the walls (one for French, one for German) and a large hexagonal table in the centre of the room which enables all the pupils to sit in a way which is conducive to involvement and participation. There is easy access to a cassette recorder, OHP and other necessary equipment.

It is important to stress that the FLA only withdraws small groups when the teacher is confident that the pupils will not take advantage of the situation. Although most classes are timetabled with the assistant at some time, it is not always appropriate or desirable for every pupil to work in small groups with the FLA away from the teacher – in many cases the model of the FLA working with the teacher in the classroom remains preferable. In consultation with the FLA, the teacher divides the class into groups of four to six pupils. These groups remain fixed so that it is possible for the FLA to withdraw them from the lesson on a rota basis. When it is considered appropriate for the assistant to withdraw groups, half the groups are taken out one week and the other half the following week. Each group spends about fifteen minutes with the FLA (lessons last 50 minutes). Both teacher and FLA keep a record of who was withdrawn and what activities were covered. The FLA accompanies each group to and from the classroom at agreed times. The activities are always organised so that no pupils miss vital teacher-led instruction when they are out of the classroom with the FLA – careful thought is given to what the rest of the class will do during the FLA lesson.

Liaison between the teacher and the FLA becomes a fairly slick process once a good working relationship has been established. When the FLA is not withdrawing groups, he or she is working alongside the teacher in the classroom and so becomes very aware of the teacher's expectations and the group's capabilities. Joint planning of the withdrawal activity can also be aided by using a framework that is transferable to a range of language topics, such as memory games, songs, twenty questions, bingo, and so on. Some time for the FLA to produce simple resources for these activities is also built into the timetable, though it is made clear to FLAs that they must expect to devote some extra time to lesson-planning as a matter of course. Good homemade resources are kept and used over and over again by subsequent assistants.

Pupils look forward to their mini-lessons with the FLA with whom they are usually on first-name terms and it is often in these sessions that a lot of worthwhile (and sometimes unplanned) language learning and real interaction take place.

Some possible small-group activities

The following games and activities lend themselves very well to the small group situation with the FLA. They have also been tried and tested by teachers and FLAs in a great number of secondary schools in the South West of England.

▪ Memory game (Pelmanism)

Pupils find pairs by remembering the cards that have been turned over, picking up two at a time from the cards laid face-down on the table. One half of the set must match the other half in some way, such as pictures to go with words.

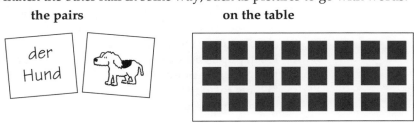

the pairs　　　　　　**on the table**

Pupils can make the cards themselves and play in pairs or as teams. Having matched the cards, they become a prompt for oral activities.

A variation with the same cards is Snap where the picture and word cards are all shuffled together, then dealt out to the players who call out a suitable target language version of the word "snap" when they see two matching cards.

▪ Telephone game

Use an old telephone (or Fisher-Price telephone if you have children!) to play a version of Pass the parcel. The FLA controls the game by passing the telephone around a group of pupils. When the FLA makes a ringing sound, the pupil holding the telephone has to "answer" it and have an impromptu conversation with the FLA who pretends to be at other end of the line. Incorrect responses and so on mean that the pupil is "out" and those left in resume the game. The dialogue can be basic or more complex, depending on the class and the individual pupil.

■ Describing a picture

The FLA sends one pupil out of the room and then shows a picture to the rest of the group. They practise how to describe what they see and when the absent pupil returns, he or she is given a pen with which to redraw the picture based only on a verbal description from the rest of the class. Comparing the two pictures can be very amusing!

■ Noughts and crosses

Draw a grid of three by three or four by four squares on the board/OHP and make some cardboard or paper circles and crosses (eight of each).

Divide the group into two teams – the circles and the crosses. They take turns to choose a square by giving its reference and then by saying in the foreign language the structure which it represents. For example, *A2: Je vais à la banque.* The FLA sticks on a circle or cross each time they get it right. The winners are the first team to get a complete line of circles or crosses.

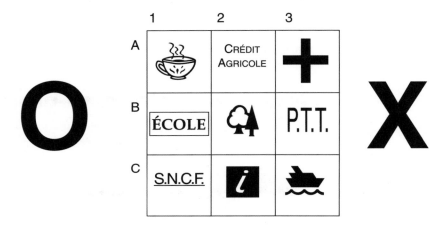

This game can be played at all levels of language. It is possible to restrict the language needed to the basic vocabulary of the pictures, or to take the exercise much further by insisting that pupils will only score points if they make correct sentences based on the picture and a particular language structure, such as the simple future tense, "I'm going to the station/park". Again, at an even higher level, pupils may be required to use structures to give advice, "You should go to the station" – or even structures that involve the subjunctive in some languages, "I have to go to the station".

Such games are versatile and can be used at any level with almost any class.

■ Desert island

Everyone in the group has a list of possible items which they may need on a desert island. The FLA divides them into pairs to discuss and decide on four items from the much longer list. Each pair must then report back to the whole group to say what they have chosen and why. The FLA listens to them all and lists the items which the groups have in common – they then decide on four items from the whole group.

Once again, this game lends itself to being played at different levels by different classes. It can be used simply to practise individual items of vocabulary in a list or to incorporate practice of the immediate future, "I'm going to take..." or to practise more complex structures such as, "If I was going to this desert island, I would take..."

The teacher and the FLA can plan exactly what aspects of the language they want pupils to practise while they are involved in the activity.

▪ Family tree

Make two family trees, one with details and one without. Working in pairs or groups, one pupil has to ask for the information and the other has to give it (name, age, job, etc.).

▪ Who am I?

One pupil thinks of a well-known personality and the rest of the group must discover the identity by asking questions about his or her life, job, interests, etc.

▪ Twenty questions

This is like the above game but the group are strictly limited to just twenty questions and the person can only reply with "Yes" or "No", so the questions have to be carefully chosen.

▪ Kim's game

This makes memory and recall of objects and language fun! The traditional version is to show a picture or a set of objects to a group for a short spell (perhaps one minute), then cover or remove all the objects and get pupils to tell you what the objects were. Some variations include:
• removing not all but only ONE or SOME of the things
• getting pupils to tell you WHERE the objects were, as well as naming them
• playing the game with words or phrases instead of objects and rubbing these off the board
• asking pupils to speak or write the answers.

▪ Comparing similar pictures

This activity is for pairs and it can be played at any level depending on the picture stimulus chosen. Find examples of "Spot The Differences" games in children's magazines and puzzle books (two similar, but not identical, pictures are given and the aim is to find a certain number of differences between the two). If you prefer, choose your own picture and make a copy of it on which you make certain small changes.

Give picture A to one pupil in the pair and picture B to the other one. They are not allowed to see each other's picture. They take turns to describe their picture to their partner, who can ask questions, such as, "Is there a chair with a book on it in the left corner?" As they give and listen to the descriptions, each pupil makes a list of what he or she thinks are the differences. As soon as one pupil thinks he or she has found the stated number of differences, the activity stops and the pupils compare the pictures.

▪ Dominoes

The fact that this is recognisable as a real game adds to the pupil involvement. The assistant can prepare for it by making up simple dominoes with a picture on one half of the card and the matching word(s) on another card.

Each pupil in the small group receives a set of dominoes – as they place them on the table, they must say what the picture is in the target language – the next player places a domino so that the writing matches the picture on the one before. If a player cannot go, he or she misses a turn. Pupils can help by making the domino cards themselves.

■ Just a minute

This is based on the well-known radio game and is best used with older pupils. One pupil is given a theme or topic and has to speak on that subject for one minute without "repetition, deviation or hesitation". If any of these rules are broken, other pupils may challenge the speaker – if the challenge is accepted by the assistant (i.e. if there really was repetition, etc.), the challenger takes over and continues speaking where the other one left off, and so on. Whoever is speaking at the end of the minute is the winner of the point. Pupils are not allowed to refer to any written notes.

■ Song reconstruction

If the assistant wants the group to learn a song, it is often a good idea to give them a gapped version of the song to refer to as they listen to it. Their task is to find the missing words. You can make the task easier by giving the pupils a list of the missing words (in the wrong order) from which they can make their choices. You may prefer to give them all the lines but in the wrong order as an alternative activity.

Further suggestions for activities are included in Appendix 4, pages 34–41.

The FLA with individuals

16-plus

You may wish to timetable your FLA to work with individual pupils on specific problems of pronunciation or grammar. This can be particularly helpful with Year 12 students who often find the change from a class of 30 pupils to a small A-level group of five or six quite challenging. We have all, no doubt, come across the perennial problem of the Year 12 "silence" – students who will not respond orally to all our best efforts at motivation. Their reluctance is often caused by a lack of confidence in their linguistic ability now that the teacher's spotlight is on them far more often than it was in the relative security of the large GCSE class. The FLA can certainly help here, but will once again need to follow clear guidance from the teacher on what strategies to employ.

Able pupils

The FLA can also contribute much to individual pupils who are already so advanced in the language that they require stretching. Working with the assistant provides an excellent authentic opportunity to enrich the language learning experience of such pupils. The FLA can help them through the use of IT, assist them in their independent reading and spend valuable time helping them to improve their speaking, listening and writing skills.

The FLA and assessment of speaking skills

A well-trained FLA can assist a teacher in the informal assessment of speaking skills. We all know how very hard it is to assess speaking in the end-of-unit tests. It is the one section that is the most often left out! It is possible for the teacher to provide the FLA with perhaps five to ten key prompts that will form the basis of a speaking assessment with individual pupils. The pupil utterances can always be marked by the FLA according to the following universal scheme:
2 points = message easily and fully understood
1 point = message understood, but with some difficulty
0 point = message not understood.
  Before the FLA can run the interviews alone, he or she will need to sit in with the teacher to observe how it should be done and to have a clear understanding

of the mark scheme. The following example has been used by the FLA in a Bristol secondary school.

YEAR 7 GERMAN SPEAKING TEST

Marks

2 = The answer or question from the pupil is correct
1 = The answer or question can be understood, but with some difficulty
0 = The answer or question is very wrong or not understandable

Teacher Questions (pupil does not see these)

1. Wie heißt du?
2. Wie schreibt man das? (Name oder Vorname)
3. Wo wohnst du?
4. Wie alt bist du?
5. Hast du Geschwister?

Pupil Questions (pupil has the following written prompts)

6. Ask the assistant's name.
7. Ask where she lives.
8. Ask if she has brothers/sisters.

Total = 8 x 2 = 16

(To assistant: Please list pupil's name, scores for each question and total score out of 16)

A class of 30 pupils can be assessed by the FLA over two lessons using the above model. The FLA assessment then becomes a further important element in the overall assessment of the student's speaking skills by the teacher and the students become used to the idea of "speaking tests" at an early age. The teacher remains in control of assessment – the FLA assists in the task.

It depends on your FLA

Ultimately, the amount of controlled freedom which you allow your FLA to enjoy in work with small groups or individuals will depend on the personality of the FLA. Some assistants will contribute more to the department working alongside the teacher in the classroom. They may not have the confidence to withdraw groups successfully and should therefore not attempt to do so. With such FLAs, small group activities can still take place, but perhaps as part of a carousel in the classroom with the teacher.

Others will come into their own if they are given a little more freedom, provided that the teacher always remains involved and retains overall control.

Summary

• Pupils can benefit from working in small groups.

• The teacher needs to retain overall control.

• Joint planning between the FLA and the teacher is necessary.

5 Special contributions by the FLA

Producing resources

All FLAs have special talents which may not necessarily be exploited in their teaching. A rather reticent assistant who is not fully at ease with children may have hidden skills in other fields such as word-processing, art or music. The FLA may leap at the opportunity to use these skills as part of the role of assistant to help the modern languages department develop its resources. You may consider allocating one period per week or per fortnight of the FLA's timetable for the production of materials. This will bring added variety to the range of tasks performed by the FLA and will be of clear benefit to the department. The teacher will need to give guidance to the FLA on what is required and for what level of pupil – awareness of differentiation is very important. There will be a strong sense of job satisfaction for the assistant who sees the tangible products of his or her work being used and valued around the department. Remember that FLAs have an entitlement to personal and professional development while they are working in the UK and that they may have their own very valid ideas on how they may achieve this.

Case study 1 – Using IT

Marlis, the Swiss-German FLA in this 11–18 Bristol school was able to do some basic word-processing but was excited to see the excellent IT facilities enjoyed by her British colleagues both in the staff quiet room and the modern languages office. She made it clear that she would like to develop her own IT skills while in the school and she learned very quickly from language colleagues how to use spreadsheets, Microsoft Publisher and other up-to-date software.

Her first resources produced for the department were a range of bilingual word lists, categorised into topics and presented in a very simple, clear format. Each list was based on a unit of *Zickzack 1*. The lists were printed in sufficient quantities for pupils to paste into their exercise books and they provided them with a useful source of reference and gave the teacher a valuable resource on which learning homeworks could be based.

Marlis went on to use IT to type gapped transcripts of songs used by the language teachers, together with up-to-date songs on CDs which she had brought from Switzerland. She transferred some of these transcripts to overhead transparencies and copied the songs from CD to cassette. She also saved the transcripts to floppy disk, enabling her colleagues to edit them in order to produce their own gapped versions to highlight other areas of vocabulary and grammar which vary according to the target class and year group. These resources still form part of a much-used bank of materials.

The FLA who has no IT experience can also be trained by colleagues and can quickly acquire the necessary skills. Other useful resources produced by Marlis on the computer included:
- large titles for displays of work
- personalised worksheets and game sheets
- information-gap activities
- model pieces of extended writing (letters, descriptions, essays)
- poetry and other forms of creative writing.

A very competent FLA will also be able to learn how to create and save new texts on the computer network that can then be used with word manipulation packages such as *Fun With Texts, Developing Tray* or *Muddles*.

Case study 2 – Supplementing library resources

The French FLA, Sylvie, was often very ill at ease in her contacts with adolescent children. After a number of problems, the head of department and mentor decided to limit her teaching time to lessons with Years 7 and 8, Year 11 and the sixth form. In consultation with Sylvie, it was agreed that the remainder of her timetable should be devoted to improving the range of language resources currently available to pupils in the school library. The FLA was delighted to be able to do this since it suited her interests and personality and meant that she could work closely with the teacher responsible for library resources with whom she had a very good relationship.

Sylvie made two very important contributions to the modern languages library reading programme. The first was her creation of a bank of cassette recordings of the short stories contained in the *Lire Davantage* series of readers published by Heinemann. She was able to record the contents of one book on one side of a C-30 cassette, thus making it very easy for pupils to access the recordings on the listening centres provided in the library studio. Language classes in the school have regular timetabled use of the library and are now able to take turns in reading and listening to the stories which they have chosen. Her recordings help the young readers in their comprehension of the text since they introduce new elements such as tone, drama and intonation.

Her second major contribution was to select stories, cartoons and articles from the previous year's Mary Glasgow magazines, mount them on to card and devise one appropriate activity to accompany the text in order to make, a) the text more accessible to the pupil and b) guide the pupil's reading of the text. She also received guidance on choosing texts of various levels of difficulty and devised a colour-coding system for the cards to help the pupils in their choice of text. The finished bank of materials looks like this:
- a row of plastic wallets suspended on a library display stand
- each plastic wallet contains
  - the original colour text, mounted on card (one copy)
  - several copies of an accompanying consumable activities sheet
  - a short "dictionary list" to aid comprehension
- each wallet is colour-coded according to difficulty.

Over her months in the school, Sylvie produced over sixty such reading packs. Many are still being used, though it is necessary to update some texts each year by "cannibalising" the previous year's Mary Glasgow magazines. It is also necessary to top up the consumable sheets at regular intervals. The activities on the sheets include the following:
- true/false questions
- multiple-choice questions
- find the French for...
- spelling games (anagrams, etc.)
- crossword puzzles
- wordsearches
- write a summary of the story/article
- closed questions (*Eric Cantona a joué pour quelles équipes françaises?*)
- gapped texts.

The example on page 22 accompanies a one-page Astérix cartoon which was aimed at Year 8 pupils. It shows how a fairly straightforward target language activity devised by the FLA can be used with an enjoyable, attractive reading text.

```
LE FILS D'ASTERIX

1. Où est le village d'Astérix?        5. Dans le rêve d'Obélix, il y a
   A en Espagne           [  ]            A une cigogne         [  ]
   B en Gaule             [  ]            B un chien            [  ]
   C à Rome               [  ]            C un chat             [  ]

2. Quelle heure est-il?                6. Astérix a un pull
   A 5 heures du matin    [  ]            A jaune               [  ]
   B 6 heures du matin    [  ]            B rouge               [  ]
   C 7 heures du matin    [  ]            C noir                [  ]

3. Quel temps fait-il?                 7. Obélix a
   A Il pleut             [  ]            A un chat             [  ]
   B Il neige             [  ]            B un chien            [  ]
   C Il fait beau         [  ]            C un poisson          [  ]

4. Quelle est la date?                 8. Dans le couffin il y a
   A lundi                [  ]            A un lapin            [  ]
   B jeudi                [  ]            B un bébé             [  ]
   C samedi               [  ]            C un oiseau           [  ]
```

Case study 3 – Story-telling and music

Philippe, the French FLA in this 11–16 Bristol comprehensive school was a practising primary school teacher in France, spending a year as an assistant for his own personal and professional development. His primary background meant that he had particular skills in story-telling which he was keen to use with his British pupils. Working closely with the head of department, Philippe devised or adapted simple (but sometimes dramatic!) stories based mainly on the language already covered by the pupils. Each class then enjoyed a fortnightly ten-minute slot during which Philippe sat down at the front of the class while the teacher became a member of the audience. Philippe then told his story, speaking very clearly, varying his voice, using mime and gesture for dramatic effect and providing some minimal musical accompaniment on the guitar. The pupils were often spell-bound and looked forward to these sessions as a special treat!

When Philippe shared his story-telling ideas with other FLAs during an INSET meeting for assistants organised by the LEA, some others were inspired to follow his example with their classes and soon many of the pupils of Bristol were listening to stories in French, German, Italian and Spanish!

The FLA with sixth form groups

An assistant will often feel quite close to your sixth-formers in terms of age, interests, youth culture, and so on. There is clearly the potential for a genuine exchange of ideas between the FLA and your A-level students who are, after all, your most advanced students in terms of linguistic skill. Close collaborative work between your sixth form language teachers and your FLAs can enable you to give the assistant a more independent and special role with the sixth-formers who will benefit from individual, pair or small group involvement with the young foreigner. Although the planning and collaboration are essential pre-requisites, once the ground has been prepared, you can entrust the FLA with a range of tasks and activities for the sixth form.

The following are some suggestions which are all designed to enrich the sixth form languages curriculum and reinforce the "normal" lessons of the classroom teacher:

- using up-to-date foreign songs, perhaps with themes relevant to A-level topics

- helping with essay planning through brainstorming of ideas, vocabulary, etc.
- preparing discussions and presentations for oral exams
- giving first-hand information about the education system
- enriching and updating vocabulary
- concentrating on aspects of literary texts through dramatic play-reading, acting out of key scenes from books, re-telling stories from another character's point of view, encouraging students to make presentations, etc.
- giving a young person's perspective of contemporary society
- setting up structured role plays based on relevant themes and topics.

The extra-curricular FLA

Your FLA will be able to contribute to the school and the languages department outside the normal curriculum. Although you must be careful not to overload the assistant (remember their contract usually stipulates twelve hours lesson time per week), it would be a pity not to involve the FLA in as many extra-curricular activities as possible. A well-integrated assistant who feels part of the team will in any case be keen to offer their support in order to enrich the pupils' foreign language learning experience.

A languages club

Some schools encourage their FLAs to run a club during the lunch break and an allowance is made for this when timetabling their lessons. Those most keen to take part are often the youngest pupils, but the club may also provide a welcome refuge for older pupils. Some of the latter (sixth-formers and Year 11 pupils perhaps) can be encouraged to help run and supervise activities as part of a team with the FLA, thus providing a nice boost for their own language skills and general confidence. Initially a teacher will need to help set up the club and will want to continue to put in regular appearances to ensure there are no problems, but there is no reason why the real responsibility for the club should not fall to the FLA, provided that he or she is confident in that role.

It might be possible to fund the languages club through the school's overall extra-curricular budget. A small grant of £150 will buy word games such as *Scrabble* and *Boggle* which can be played in any language, foreign language versions of *Cluedo* and *Monopoly* and perhaps some Mini-Flashcard Games.

The normal resources of the languages department can also be used to good effect by the languages club as follows:

- using computer software
- watching a foreign language film (over two lunch breaks)
- planning, performing and filming a sketch
- making things from instructions in the foreign language.

The FLA may wish to take the club members elsewhere in the school to use other resources, such as food technology in order to follow a recipe, or just to use the additional space for treasure hunts and other games. It is advisable to check that any Health and Safety issues have been addressed and that the FLA's involvement in any such activities in a supervisory role is approved by the senior management team.

The interaction fostered by the languages club between FLA and pupils will be mutually beneficial to all concerned.

Intensive language sessions

Your FLA may help you to improve FL2 provision within your school. This area of the curriculum often suffers the "squeeze" effect of a National Curriculum which insists on a large number of core and foundation subjects for pupils. In many schools, FL2 has become a "twilight" activity for teachers and pupils and is taught in perhaps just one session per week – hardly allowing for the regular, repeated lessons which give the optimum framework for language learning.

In exchange for being temporarily relieved of some lessons within the normal school day, the assistant can take responsibility for an intensive two-hour session after school with the FL2 group. Alternatively, the FL2 group could be asked to attend school on part of an INSET day, to be taught by the FLA instead of their normal teacher. The Central Bureau guidelines allow for this but only with small groups and with the express agreement of the FLA, who should not feel under any pressure to take on a responsibility which he or she would rather not have. In all such cases, joint planning and preparation by the FLA and teacher would be essential and a member of staff would need to be on hand should the FLA require assistance. This would not be difficult to arrange and would be very worthwhile for the pupils concerned. Such sessions would benefit pupils from all years. A possible framework for an intensive session in the run-up to the GCSE examination could be based entirely on one or two weak topic areas and might include:
• a listening task
• several speaking tasks (role play and general conversation)
• back-up work with a schools television programme (*Ici Paris, Lernexpress*)
• some IT work (for reading and writing)
• language games.

Feedback from both parents and pupils after such sessions is always very encouraging and there is no doubt that this can be an important strategy for improving examination performance by providing a much-needed boost at the best possible time.

Visits to local languages events

If you are lucky enough to live in an area where foreign language films are shown at the cinema, where the local ALL or educational institutions organise lectures and seminars for language students or where university language departments put on foreign language plays for schools, you would do well to consider booking one extra place at these events so that your FLA can join the teacher and students. This extra-curricular involvement by the assistant will then make it possible for him or her to play a more meaningful part in any preparatory or follow-up activities in school. The same is true of visits abroad but REMEMBER: the FLA is not a qualified teacher and cannot be expected to assume the responsibilities of qualified teachers on any school visits.

Other departments in the school may also wish to invite the FLA to accompany them on their museum visits or field trips, and this can do much to enhance the assistant's relationship with both pupils and colleagues as well as give him or her opportunities to get to know Britain and aspects of our education system better.

Extra-curricular writing

Some assistants arrive in their UK schools with ideas for exchanges of correspondence with schools in their home country. Once a link has been established, the FLA can play an important part in helping the British pupils to write to their foreign penfriends or even helping them to decipher the special characteristics of the French, German or Spanish handwriting!

Creative writing is also an area for which the FLA may wish to take some responsibility. The assistant could, for example, be on hand to help pupils in the re-drafting stage of writing a poem, suggesting other possible words or drawing their attention to inaccuracies. This may occur naturally in the FLA's role of working alongside the teacher when the classroom focus is on the production of a piece of creative writing. It may also be possible to send small groups of pupils to the FLA in order to allow them to concentrate on their writing away from the rest of the class.

The finished product may be displayed on the classroom wall or may be part of the school's entry in one of the now regular creative writing competitions organised by publishers or local language associations. Whatever the case, the FLA can make a valuable and authentic input into this important area of language enrichment. The language learned in the process is often remembered by the pupils for many years.

A languages show

An assistant with a flair for drama, music, poetry or dance can play a vital part in the preparation and organisation of a "languages show" which would take the form of an evening of entertainment for parents and pupils.

Case study

Lise, the French assistant in this 11–18 South Gloucestershire school, wanted to put on a show for parents. Over a six-week period, she used all her lessons to coach groups of pupils and individuals in a range of performances including songs, dance, poetry and homemade sketches. Teachers from the languages department were also involved, together with the German assistant, Volker. Pupils participating were also given two mornings "off timetable" for final rehearsals. The end result was an excellent display of talent from pupils of all ages which provided a real boost for the languages department and was also a very good advertisement for the school. A lot of commitment from the FLAs was essential since they were the key sources of inspiration for the pupils. They also had the added advantage of being able to provide music and songs from the contemporary youth cultures of their countries.

Summary

- The FLA can enrich the languages curriculum outside the classroom.

- FLAs need an opportunity to exploit their talents.

- The teacher must trust and support the FLA.

Putting the case for FLAs

Appendix 1

The following are extracts from a flyer circulated to schools by the National Association of Language Advisers. You may find persuasive arguments to use with your headteacher and governors.

FOREIGN LANGUAGE ASSISTANTS

Who are they?

Young overseas students or recent graduates, the majority studying English, who elect to come to the United Kingdom as part of their Higher Education course.

What are their conditions of service?

The period of appointment is from October 1st to May 31st. The cost of employing an assistant in 1996/97 was £4,900 inclusive of employer's National Insurance contributions. Assistants and costs may be shared between institutions. The work required of them will not normally exceed twelve hours per week. However, at the request of the school and with the agreement of the assistant, they may work some additional hours provided they are offered on a pro-rata basis.

What do they do?

They offer invaluable support to language learners by:

■ providing opportunities for pupils to hear a young native speaker, thereby stimulating genuine classroom communication

■ assisting the teacher in the classroom (group work, role play) or working with small groups of pupils away from the classroom

■ enabling more pupils to take part in individual conversations in the foreign language

■ bringing, by their very presence, the foreign country and its culture into the classroom.

How do they help the Modern Languages department?

■ They provide invaluable oral practice for both teaching and testing.

■ They share in the task of assessing pupils' progress.

■ They act as a model speaker to facilitate classroom demonstrations.

■ They produce authentic resources for use in the classroom.

■ They bring printed and recorded materials from their country.

Why do schools and colleges need them?

■ All examinations, including GCSE, AS and A levels, emphasise the importance of oral performance.

■ Modern languages are best taught through practical communication.

■ Pupils need contact with young native speakers.

■ Resources and teaching styles are enriched.

■ Teachers need regular contact with native speakers to update their own knowledge of the target language and culture.

■ Schools need all possible support to meet the demands of the National Curriculum in Modern Languages.

■ Schools are deeply concerned with the personal and social development of all their pupils.

■ Schools must help pupils relate positively to people from other language backgrounds and different cultures.

■ Schools need to offer a curriculum which provides an international dimension and prepares pupils for European citizenship.

A checklist of items for the FLA   Appendix 2

The following is a checklist of items which the FLA could
bring from his or her home country for use in teaching.

FOREIGN LANGUAGE ASSISTANT CHECKLIST

- School timetables

- School reports

- School meals menu for the week

- School brochures

- School stationery (homework diary, etc.)

- Cassettes and CDs with transcriptions of songs

- Video and radio recordings (news, pop charts, soaps, etc.)

- Teenage magazines

- Newspapers and current affairs magazines

- Brochures and maps of their area

- Information about sports in their home town

- Special offer posters and leaflets from shops

- Realia such as bus tickets, cinema programmes, advertising flyers, timetables

- Photos of home neighbourhood and school

- Information about possible penfriend links

- Addresses of schools and colleges in home town

- Video recordings of television adverts

- Examples of foreign currency and postage stamps

- Menus from cafés and restaurants

- Cartoons

- Postcards

- Mail order catalogues

- Forms from the post office and banks

- Simple weather forecasts

Reviewing progress

The following Review and Summary sheets should be
read in conjunction with Chapter 2.

FOREIGN LANGUAGE ASSISTANT: REVIEW SHEET 1

For completion before end of Autumn term

NAME OF ASSISTANT	HEAD OF DEPARTMENT/MENTOR

A. YOUR LANGUAGE TEACHING

AREAS FOR REVIEW	NOTES
1 How do you feel your lessons are going?	
2 Do the pupils understand you in your language?	
3 Do you think the pupils enjoy your lessons?	
4 Does your timetable present any problems for you?	
5 Are you able to discuss your work with colleagues?	
6 Do you get the support that you need?	
7 Are you able to get the equipment/resources you need?	
8 Are there other contributions you could make to the department?	
9 Do you have any other comments or concerns related to your teaching?	
10 Does working in more than one school create any special problems?	

FOREIGN LANGUAGE ASSISTANT: SUMMARY SHEET 1

For completion before end of Autumn term

AGREED STATEMENT OF PROGRESS

A

_____

_____

_____

B

_____

_____

_____

C

_____

_____

_____

PROPOSED ACTION

By school

_____

_____

_____

_____

By assistant

_____

_____

_____

_____

_____

Signed and dated
ASSISTANT

Signed and dated
HoD/MENTOR

FOREIGN LANGUAGE ASSISTANT: REVIEW SHEET 2

For completion before end of Spring term

NAME OF ASSISTANT	HEAD OF DEPARTMENT/MENTOR

ACTION SINCE PREVIOUS REVIEW

AREAS FOR REVIEW	NOTES
1 By school	
2 By assistant	

A. YOUR LANGUAGE TEACHING

AREAS FOR REVIEW	NOTES
1 Are you happy with your work over the last months?	
2 What do you feel are your own particular strengths?	
3 Are you able to discuss your work with colleagues?	
4 Do you get the support you need?	
5 Are you able to get the equipment/resources that you need?	

FOREIGN LANGUAGE ASSISTANT: SUMMARY SHEET 2

For completion before end of Spring term

AGREED STATEMENT OF PROGRESS

A
_____
_____
_____

B
_____
_____
_____

C
_____
_____
_____

PROPOSED ACTION

By school
_____
_____
_____
_____
_____

By assistant
_____
_____
_____
_____
_____

Signed and dated ASSISTANT	Signed and dated HoD/MENTOR

FOREIGN LANGUAGE ASSISTANT: FINAL EVALUATION

For completion at end of May

NAME OF ASSISTANT	HEAD OF DEPARTMENT/MENTOR

ACTION SINCE PREVIOUS REVIEW

AREAS FOR REVIEW	NOTES
1 By school	
2 By assistant	

A. YOUR LANGUAGE TEACHING

AREAS FOR REVIEW	NOTES
1 Have you enjoyed your work over the last year?	
2 What special contribution do you feel you have made?	
3 Did you feel that you were integrated into the department?	
4 Do you feel you have been able to do your job effectively?	
5 Have you been able to get the equipment/ resources that you need?	

FOREIGN LANGUAGE ASSISTANT: FINAL EVALUATION

For completion at end of May

AGREED STATEMENT OF PROGRESS

A
_____
_____
_____

B
_____
_____
_____

C
_____
_____
_____

FURTHER COMMENTS

By school
_____
_____
_____
_____

By assistant
_____
_____
_____
_____
_____

N.B. Remember to return borrowed books, room key, etc.

Signed and dated ASSISTANT	Signed and dated HoD/MENTOR

1. TRUE OR FALSE

Aim: Vocabulary practice

Skills: Aural comprehension

Level: Any level

Equipment: None

The assistant has a competition against the group or class by making statements related to the language point being practised. If what the FLA says is true, a member of the class should say so:
"You buy bread in a baker's" = True.
When the statement is false, the pupils must spot this:
"You buy fish in a theatre" = False.

Decide on how to score the game beforehand. For example, if the class gets five correct answers in five minutes, they win one point but if they fail to reach this target, the FLA gets a point and the first to reach ten points wins. The pupils can also take over from the FLA and give the statements themselves.

2. PLANNING A TRIP ABROAD

Aim: Simulate organising a visit abroad

Skills: Oral, collaborative, phoning, organising, information retrieval

Level: Good Year 11 or sixth-formers

Equipment: Phones, tourist brochures

In this activity, the FLA plays the role of travel agent or employee in a tourist information office. The pupils' task is to find out certain pieces of information from the assistant in order to plan their holiday or business trip in the foreign country.

The pupils are told they have a certain budget and are given dates for their journey. They are issued with leaflets (authentic if possible) about the area and their job is to have a simulated phone conversation with the FLA, who has more detailed information than the pupils (hotel prices, availability, opening times).

If possible, the school's internal phone system could be used for added authenticity. If a database is available, this could also be used as the source of the detailed information.

3. PICTURES ON AN OHP

Aim: Oral practice

Skills: Oral, questioning skills

Level: All levels but mainly younger pupils

Equipment: OHP and pens, OHTs, books from which to copy cartoon characters

Obviously the FLA will need an OHP for teaching and as these are such versatile pieces of equipment, it would make sense to allow the FLA easy access to one. Pictures can be drawn on to transparencies in order to practise structures and vocabulary at a very basic or complex level of language. Pictures can be photocopied from books such as the the MGP *Timesavers* collection in French, German or Spanish.

Example 1: Copy a picture of a house with a cut-away view of the rooms and their furniture. On a smaller piece of OHT, copy a cartoon character and then move this around the house, getting pupils to describe the positions. Make several characters for variety. Extend the language by getting pupils to refer to furniture: "He's in the sitting room, between the TV and the armchair".

Example 2: Put a picture on the OHP and use the focus control to move it out of focus. Gradually turn the control to bring it slowly back into focus. As the FLA does this, the pupils guess what the picture represents and they build up a correct description of it.

Example 3: The FLA uses pieces of paper to cover parts of the picture. He or she gradually moves the paper to reveal more of the picture. The pupils guess what is still covered and describe the picture.

Example 4: Using small objects, animals or people cut from OHTs, construct an event on the screen such as a street in which something is about to happen (car accident, robbery). Move the objects and people around the screen to suggest that there is movement and the incident is about to take place. Then freeze the scene and get pupils to speculate as to what will happen next. Try out their various scenarios on the screen, or let them come out and do it for you.

4. SPELLING

Aim: Oral practice of alphabet and spelling

Skills: Listening, spelling, collaboration

Level: Basic

Equipment: Two sets of the alphabet on cards, Blu-Tack

Make two sets of 26 large cards each showing a letter of the alphabet. Divide the group into two and select pairs of pupils (one from each team) to compete. Place the letters on the floor or stick them on the walls.

The FLA calls out a word (country, transport, etc.) and the two pupils rush around gathering the letters that make up the word and getting team members to hold up the cards in the correct order.

For real fun, get the team members to stand so that the cards are in the same order as the letters in the words. Where the same letter occurs more than once, the team member holding that letter moves down the line to show where the letter occurs. The winning team is the first one to spell the word correctly. The next two players then take responsibility for the next word.

5. CATEGORIES GAME

Aim: Vocabulary practice and enrichment

Skills: Listening, writing

Level: Basic to intermediate

Equipment: Pens, pencils, paper

The FLA gives a group a list of headings, such as town, country, animal, vegetable, job, first name and drink. Pupils copy them down as column headings. The FLA then picks a letter at random and pupils are given a time limit in which to write as many words as they can in the different categories beginning with the chosen letter.

At the end of the set time, each pupil calls out his/her words. The others have to listen carefully and compare the words with their own list. Pupils score one point for a correct word and two points for a correct word that nobody else had.

6. GUESS THE PHOTO

Aim: To describe a visual

Skills: Questioning, listening, oral

Level: All levels

Equipment: Large photos from magazines

The assistant has a large photo, such as a person, a landscape, the interior of a room, depending upon the complexity of the language at the group's disposal. The FLA keeps the photo hidden from the group and invites them (in turn as individuals or pairs) to speculate as to what might be in the photo. Only "Yes/No" answers are given.

At the end of a given time – or when someone has made a good guess at what is in the photo – the FLA reveals it to the group, who may then go on to describe it more fully or accurately.

7. MURDER

Aim: To describe a physical appearance

Skills: Oral communication, listening

Level: Years 7–9

Equipment: None

The FLA sends a pupil out of the room for one minute while another pupil is chosen as MURDERER! The pupil outside the room is then called back as DETECTIVE.

The detective asks the pupils questions about their physical appearance. The murderer has to lie in answer to these questions, so that once the detective discovers a lie, he/she has also discovered the murderer!
1) Suspects are only allowed to answer "Yes/No" to "closed" questions: "Is your hair black?"
2) Suspects should give fuller answers to more open questions: "What colour is your hair?" "My hair is black."

Language games and activities   Appendix 4.3

8. LOSS OF MEMORY

Aim: To create a fictitious identity and situation from "evidence"

Skills: Collaborative, creative, oral, listening

Level: Good Year 9 or above

Equipment: Variety of realia, OHP

The FLA has a carefully planned range of realia such as a rail ticket, bill, tourist leaflet, menu, and timetable. The assistant tells the group that these items have been found by the police in the pockets/handbag of a person discovered lying in the street suffering from amnesia.

The FLA divides the group into teams and each team is given a set time in which to piece together the clues in order to invent a story to explain the person's identity and to explain what he/she was doing at the time of their "accident".

The realia or clues can be photocopied on to OHT or worksheets so that everyone can see them. After a set time has elapsed, the FLA listens to each group giving their version of the story. This can be very amusing and gives great scope for imagination and creativity.

9. SALES TALK

Aim: To describe objects in great detail

Skills: Oral communication

Level: Good linguists in Year 10 and above

Equipment: Household objects

The assistant brings into school a selection of household objects, such as a torch, bottle opener, etc. He or she gives one to each pair or small group of pupils, telling them to imagine they are salesmen and women attempting to describe and sell their object to the rest of the class. They have to describe what it is used for, its advantages, why it is a good product, etc.

For a variation, the "salesperson" keeps the object hidden from view while describing its qualities and functions, so that the group also has to guess what it is.

10. ALPHABET GAMES

Aim: To practise the alphabet and spelling

Skills: Spelling, listening

Level: All levels

Equipment: Writing materials

Encourage the assistant to practise the alphabet in the foreign language as often as possible. Games for this include:
1) FLA spells words to the group which pupils have to listen to and identify.
2) Words are spelled backwards and then identified.
3) Pupils take over and spell words to each other.
4) Spell names of well-known people and places.
5) Pupils spell their own names and street names to "foreign visitors".

11. CHINESE WHISPERS

Aim: To pass a message

Skills: Listening, speaking, memory

Level: All levels

Equipment: None

The assistant writes a message on a piece of paper and shows it to a pupil who has one minute to memorise it. He/she gives the paper back to the FLA and whispers the message to a neighbour who then whispers it to the next pupil and so on right round the group.

The last pupil in the "chain" must relay the final message back to the assistant – comparing the original with the final version is great fun!

12. SENTENCE CONSTRUCTION

Aim: To practise language in a chosen topic

Skills: Reading, acting

Level: Younger pupils

Equipment: Card, scissors, envelopes

The FLA prepares the component words of sentences by writing the sentences on card and then cutting them up into individual words (or parts of words). The components are then put into an envelope. Each envelope contains the components of more than one sentence on the chosen theme, such as leisure activities:
* I watch television.
* I listen to music.
* I play on my computer.

The group is divided into teams and each team is given an envelope of cut-up sentences.

The FLA begins the game by miming an activity. The pupils' task is to select the correct cards and to construct the sentence on their desks to illustrate this activity. The FLA goes round to check progress and the first team to make a correct sentence wins a point. The FLA then chooses a pupil to mime the next action, and so on.

13. PHONE NUMBERS

Aim: To understand phone numbers

Skills: Listening, counting, speaking

Level: All years up to Year 11

Equipment: Number cards

Pupils often find the foreign language versions of phone numbers difficult, so why not play a game to practise them?

Divide the group into teams and give each team a set of number cards on which are a selection of one and two-digit numbers. The assistant calls out an imaginary phone number (and also writes it down as a check) and the first team to hold up the component cards with the digits in the correct order wins the game.

Also encourage pupils to say the numbers back to the FLA as further practice. When giving out the cards, it is best to ensure that every pupil receives at least one card so that they all have the opportunity to participate.

After a while, pupils can call out the numbers and the FLA is released to ensure fair play.

14. WHERE AM I?

Aim: To follow directions on a map

Skills: Listening, following instructions, oral

Level: All years up to Year 11

Equipment: Town plans (authentic or made)

For this, the FLA needs to give each member of the group an identical street plan of a town (use a real leaflet if possible from the FLA's home town).

The assistant begins by giving directions to a particular place (making clear, of course, where the starting point is). The pupils follow the directions with their fingers on the page and try to guess which place the assistant is going to.

The person who guesses correctly takes over from the FLA and the rest of the class follows the new instructions.

It is perhaps simplest to have the same starting point each time, though it can be varied to make the game more challenging.

15. SHOPPING

Aim: To simulate shopping

Skills: Reading, oral, listening, questioning

Level: All years up to Year 11

Equipment: Shopping lists, information lists

Divide the group into shoppers and shopkeepers. Give the shoppers a different list each. They must go around the "shops" (tables manned by shopkeepers) and find out information about the items on their list (price, size, weight, how many in a packet).

Each shopkeeper has an information list for some items, but no person (apart from the FLA) has the complete list of all items on the shoppers' lists.

To make it more fun, a shopkeeper may have the item, such as a blue hat, but not in the same colour as on the list (i.e. a green hat). The disappointed shopper must then move on to the next shop.

As pupils finish, they hand completed lists to the assistant who notes the time taken and quickly marks them. The winner is announced at the end. A variation is to tell the shopkeepers that they have sold out of an item chosen at random (fish, pens etc.).

16. CHAIN SENTENCE

Aim: To remember and add to a sentence

Skills: Listening, speaking, memory

Level: All levels

Equipment: None

Each pupil repeats the beginning of a sentence, such as "When I'm rich, I will buy..." Each pupil then adds an item to the sentence and also repeats what has gone before. In this way the sentence gets progressively longer and the memory (and linguistic) challenge becomes more difficult.

For a variation:
* add a new item PLUS an adjective
* add something from a category stipulated by the FLA (a drink/something beginning with R)
* make it into a team game
* provide pictures or flashcards to jog memory.

17. GUESS THE MISSING WORDS

Aim: To complete a gapped text

Skills: Collaborative, speaking, reading

Level: All levels

Equipment: OHP/board, worksheet

Show the group a text with a number of words blanked-out (use the board, OHP, photocopied sheet, computer screen, etc.). The FLA splits the group into two teams and they take it in turns to try to guess a missing word as the assistant writes the correct words in the text.

This often works well with short newspaper articles describing everyday incidents or accidents.

18. HANDWRITING

Aim: To understand foreign handwriting

Skills: Reading

Level: All levels

Equipment: Writing and display materials

Your FLA can provide first-hand examples of authentic foreign handwriting, so capitalise on this to obtain a range of samples in letters, OHP work, reading materials, stories and games.

This could form the basis for a classroom display and the FLA may be able to get even more samples from friends, relatives and so on.

19. WEATHER CARD GAME

Aim: To match descriptions with symbols

Skills: Reading, comprehension

Level: Years 8–11

Equipment: Large "weather map", large weather symbols, Blu-Tack, small weather maps, 24 weather description cards

This game makes weather vocabulary enjoyable to learn and teaches pupils more about the geography of the country. It also gives authentic opportunities to use the future tense, if desired.

The assistant shows the group a large map of the country with place names in bold and weather symbols beside them (use Blu-Tack to stick symbols on to make them mobile). Using repetition and question/answer, the FLA practises how to describe the weather.

The group is then divided into groups of four and each of these sub-groups is given a small weather map which is a smaller version of the large map with weather symbols pre-printed next to the towns. In the centre of their table, each group is given a pile of 24 cards containing statements about the weather in the various towns or regions: "It's going to rain in Barcelona". Pupils collect the cards that go with their maps. Each pupil takes it in turn to pick up the top card and if it matches their map, they keep it; if not, they put it to the bottom of the pile. They read the sentence from the card. The winner is the first pupil to have collected all their relevant cards.

20. WEATHER BINGO

Aim: To understand weather and places

Skills: Listening, map reading

Level: Years 8–11

Equipment: Small weather maps, small pieces of blank card

Instead of numbers, the pupils' bingo cards are small maps illustrated with weather symbols – no two cards have exactly the same combinations of places and weather. Pupils also have small pieces of card with which to cover the items that have been called out.

The FLA is the caller and calls out different combinations of weather and places until a pupil has covered all of his or her symbols. It is important for the FLA to keep a record of what has been called out so that he or she can check the accuracy of the winning cards.

21. NEWS BULLETINS

Aim: To improve comprehension of news

Skills: Listening

Level: Good Year 10 up to A-level

Equipment: Cassette and cassette recorder, possibly TV and video

The FLA can be asked to monitor the news and produce simplified versions for certain classes and advanced versions for the real linguists. This can be recorded and used by the teacher as a way of bringing variety into the lesson – the bulletins can become a regular slot in lessons to be exploited as a different form of listening activity.

A variation is the "silent video": record the British news from television and ask the FLA to make an audio cassette of the same news items in the target language. Play the video to the class with the sound turned off while the FLA's version is played on a cassette recorder.

It is interesting and amusing to see British programmes converted into a foreign language, though the FLA has to be careful with the synchronisation of sound and picture.

22. TONGUE TWISTERS

Aim: To work on pronunciation

Skills: Listening, memory, creativity

Level: Good Year 10 up to A-level

Equipment: Cassette recorder

Ask the assistant to record examples of tongue twisters and then exploit them with the pupils. The FLA could work with pupils to invent their own tongue twisters in the target language.

23. THE STATEMENT GAME

Aim: To stimulate a discussion on a topic

Skills: Oral, debating, listening

Level: Sixth form

Equipment: Statement cards, name cards

This is a very good way of providing a firm framework for a discussion with students who are reluctant or unable to participate in response to open questions.

Write a list of ten or so deliberately provocative or controversial statements on a topic in the target language: "Immigration should be halted immediately".

The FLA works with small groups of perhaps five or six. Each group is given the statements (face-down) on the table and a set of blank cards on which each student writes their name. One person turns over a statement and the group members place their name cards a) close to it if they agree, and b) further from it if they disagree.

Students are not allowed to "pass" and once all the cards have been placed, each student justifies/defends his or her opinion to the rest of the group.

Have a time limit on the discussion of each statement and get a different student to open each discussion.

24. DRAW A MONSTER

Aim: To describe a physical appearance

Skills: Listening, speaking, drawing

Level: Younger pupils

Equipment: Drawing equipment and paper

The teacher and FLA prepare a bank of descriptive phrases – the level of difficulty can vary. The FLA then dictates the phrases to the pupils who are ready to draw what they hear.

When the pictures are finished, the pupils may be asked to describe what they have drawn back to the FLA and rest of group.

Pupils may be asked to prepare their own monsters at home and then describe them to the group themselves.

25. ODD ONE OUT

Aim: To practise and enrich vocabulary

Skills: Listening, reading

Level: All levels

Equipment: OHP/flip-chart/board

This is a well-known game that can be used to practise and revise vocabulary in topics.

The group is divided into teams and the FLA then gives three or four items of vocabulary, one of which does not belong with the others. Each team must try to spot the odd one out and say why.

The FLA may call out the groups of words as a listening task or have them already prepared on flip-chart, board or OHP.

Language games and activities

26. ANSWERS & QUESTIONS

Aim: To practise questions and answers

Skills: Reading, matching, writing, speaking

Level: All years up to Year 11

Equipment: Photocopied lists of "answers"

The FLA writes a list of twenty answers and photocopies the list.

Two groups of pupils each have a list and their task is to work out twenty questions to go with the answers already provided.

This can be done orally or in writing and the level of difficulty can vary according to the class.

27. WHAT'S IN THE BAG?

Aim: To practise and enrich vocabulary

Skills: Speaking, collaborative, memory

Level: Younger pupils

Equipment: Objects, bag

The FLA brings a bag into the room containing a selection of objects which the pupils cannot see. Their task is to guess what the items are.

The items may be simple classroom objects, household objects or realia such as menus and tickets.

The FLA should give clues to prompt the class. As each item is "discovered" it is taken out of the bag and put on show.

When all the items have been seen, they can be put back in the bag and the task is now to remember and re-name all the objects in a Kim's game.

28. NEWSPAPER GAME

Aim: To encourage fast reading skills

Skills: Listening, reading

Level: Good Year 10 to sixth form

Equipment: Copies of foreign newspaper

Encourage the FLA to obtain several copies of the same edition of a local newspaper from his or her home town. He or she should also prepare some questions in advance based on various articles in the paper: "What happened to Herr Braun's cat last Tuesday?"

Divide the group into two teams, giving each team copies of the newspaper so that all team members are able to see it. The FLA then reads out the questions and the first team to find the correct answer by flicking through the pages wins a point. More points can be awarded for harder questions.

29. MAGIC THREES

Aim: To practise numbers

Skills: Listening, ability to count quickly

Level: Younger pupils

Equipment: None

The FLA explains that pupils in the group are going to count aloud, starting from one. Each time they come to a multiple of THREE, instead of saying the number, they must say a "magic word" in the target language – this can be a word of the FLA's choosing, such as *banane*, *Schildkröte*, *trattorìa*.

For some variations:
1) start counting from a higher number
2) use different multiples (for example, five instead of three)
3) count backwards.

The following extracts are taken from a flyer published by the Central Bureau.

appointment of

LINGUA ASSISTANTS
IN THE UK

OBJECTIVES OF THE PROGRAMME

One of the provisions of the European Union SOCRATES programme, Lingua Action C, involves the appointment of prospective teachers from EU Member States and from countries in the European Economic Area (EEA) as assistants in schools and colleges in the United Kingdom. EU assistants are appointed to contribute to the European dimension in the curriculum and may also assist with language teaching.

In order to avoid overlap with the existing foreign language assistants scheme, **French,- German-, Spanish- and Italian-speaking assistants will <u>not</u> be placed in secondary or post-secondary institutions where these languages are already taught.**

ROLE OF THE ASSISTANT

Upon arrival at the host institution, the assistant, in agreement with the supervising teacher, will establish a work programme covering the whole duration of the stay and setting out the tasks to be accomplished. In close collaboration with and under the supervision of a qualified teacher, the tasks to which an assistant may contribute include notably:

> improving pupils' and teachers' comprehension in the assistant's language;

> special monitoring of pupils with foreign language learning difficulties;

> disseminating information on the socio-cultural situation in the assistant's home country of origin;

> producing teaching material;

> using new technologies in the teaching of foreign languages;

> introducing or reinforcing the European dimension;

> preparing or implementing a Joint Educational Project between the host institution and an institution from the assistant's home country;

> assisting with the organisation of visits to or from a partner school.

Such activities provide assistants with experience of foreign language teaching. They should also try to improve their knowledge of the host country, its language and its educational system. Throughout the course of their duties, assistants should be fully integrated into school life.

PARTICIPATING COUNTRIES

Assistants are available from the following countries: Austria, Belgium, Denmark, Finland, France, Germany, Greece, Iceland, Italy, Liechtenstein, Luxembourg, the Netherlands, Norway, Portugal, Spain and Sweden. In 1997/98, Lingua Assistants may also be available from Bulgaria, Cyprus, the Czech Republic, Hungary, Malta, Poland, Romania and Slovakia.

Further reading

N.A.L.A and Central Bureau *The Foreign Language Assistant – A Guide To Good Practice*, Central Bureau

Working Together – Training Video and Teacher's Guide for Schools and FLAs, Channel 4 Schools

Notes for Foreign Language Assistants, Central Bureau

Notes for Schools and Colleges receiving Foreign Language Assistants, Central Bureau

Language Games and Activities, Langran and Purcell, C.I.L.T. 1994

Are You Sitting Comfortably? Young Pathfinder 3, C.I.L.T.

On Target: Teaching in the Target Language Pathfinder 5, C.I.L.T.

Using the Target Language Concepts 1, C. Macdonald, MGP

Working With Your Student Teacher Concepts 5, Calvert and Fletcher, MGP

Appointment of Lingua Assistants in the UK, Central Bureau

Working with your Foreign Language Assistant – A Handbook for Schools, Leeds Education Advisory and Inspection Services (Tel. 0113 214 4068)

La boîte à utils de l'assistant de français au Royaume-Uni, French Embassy

Praktische Unterrichtstips für Assistenten im Vereinigten Königreich, Goethe Institut

Actividades para la clase de español elaboradas por auxiliares de conversación, Spanish Embassy